Mandalas Coloring Book for Teens
Stress Less Coloring

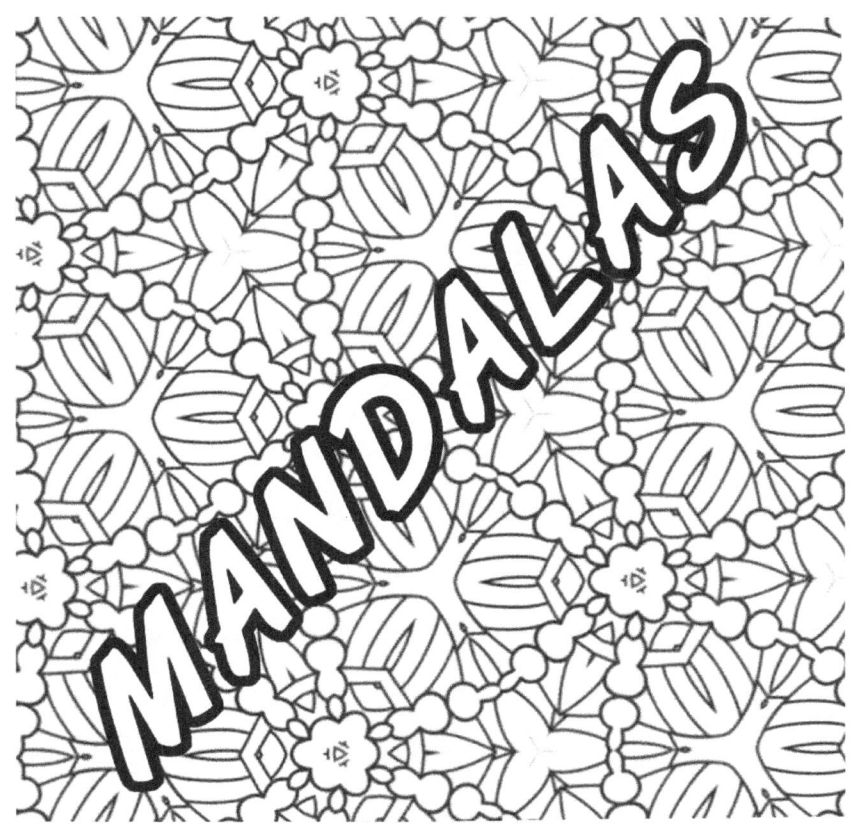

Jasmine Andrews

Mandalas Coloring Book for Teens
Stress Less Coloring

ISBN-13: 978-1542744881

ISBN-10: 1542744881

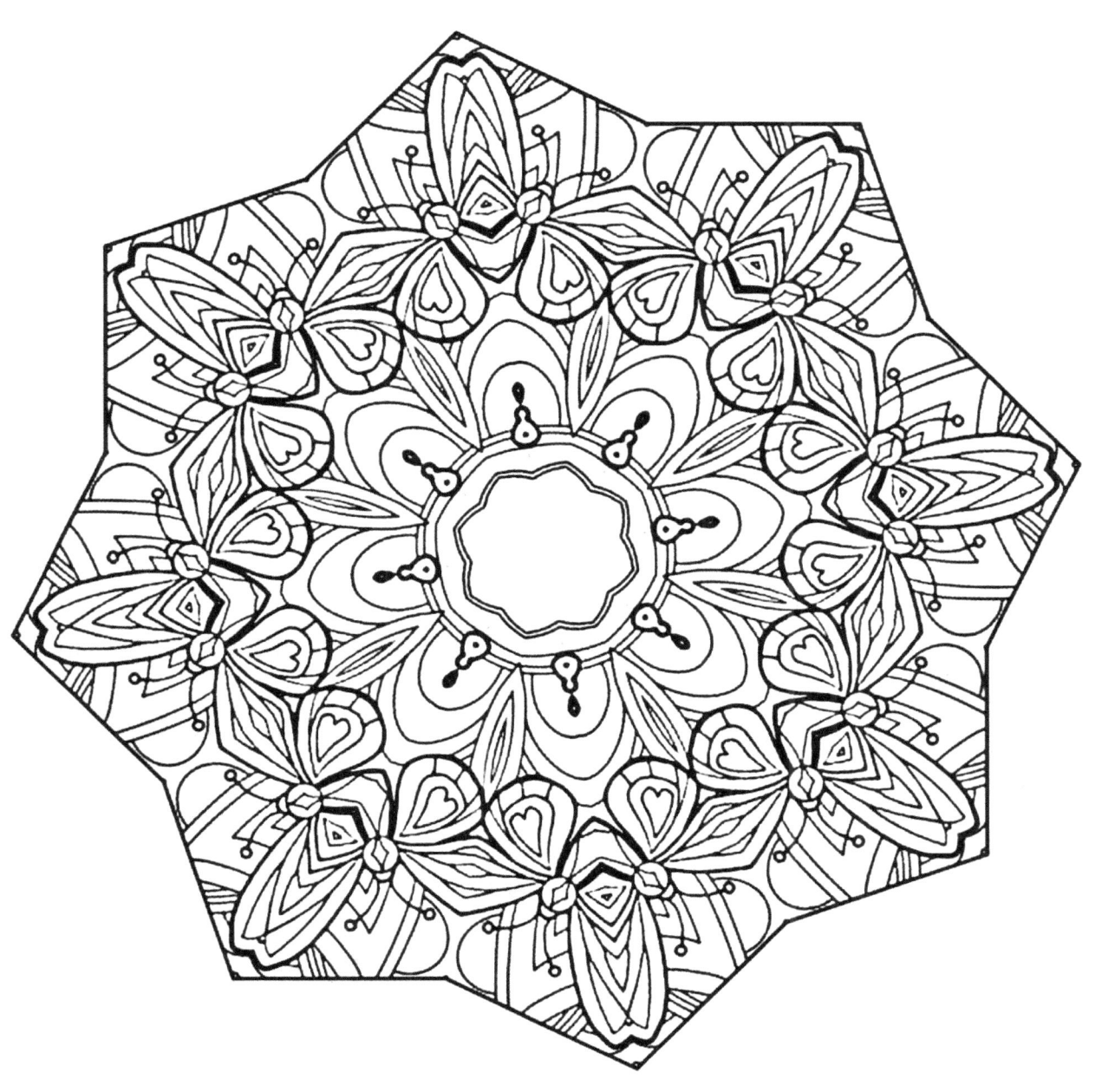

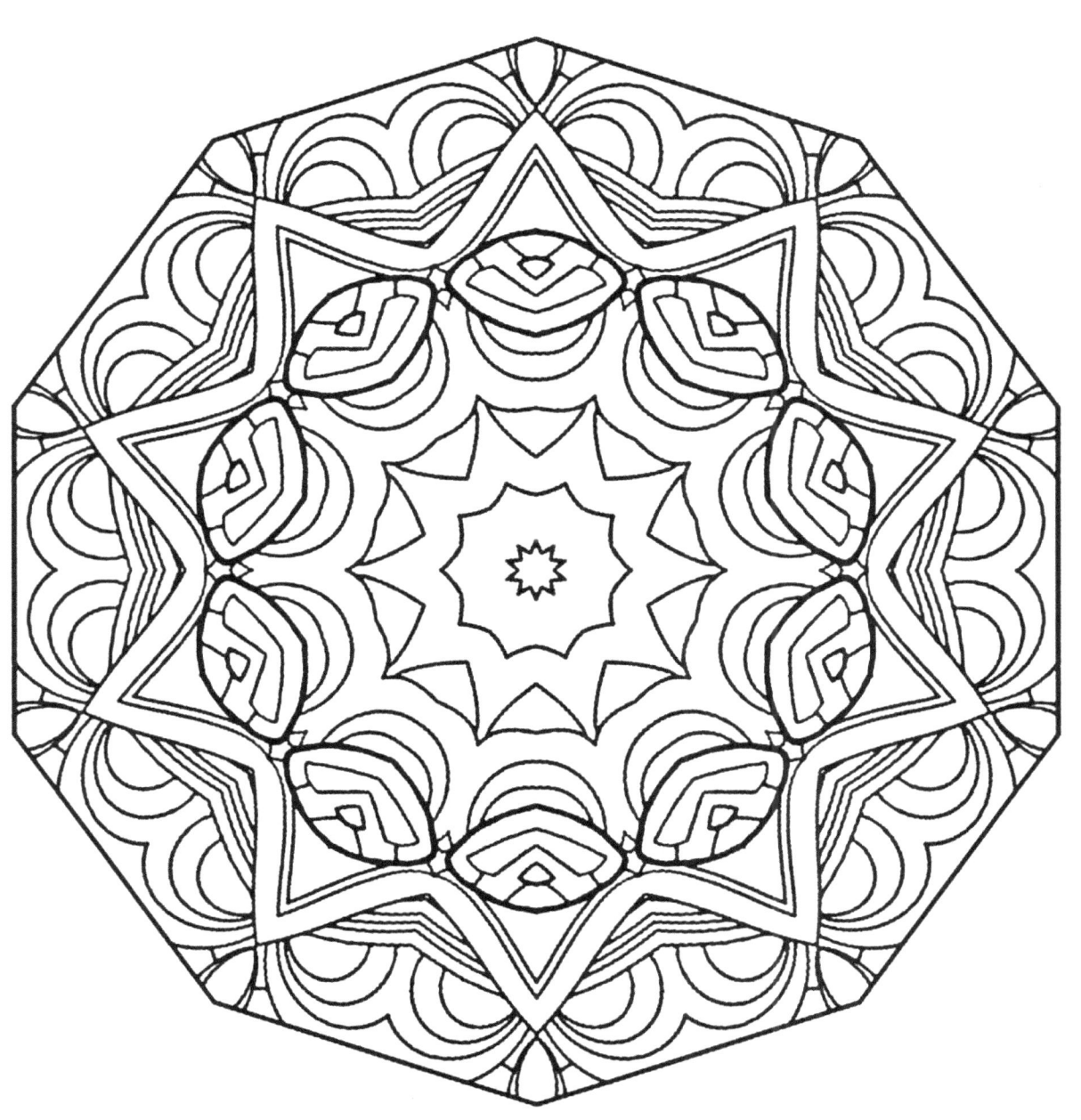

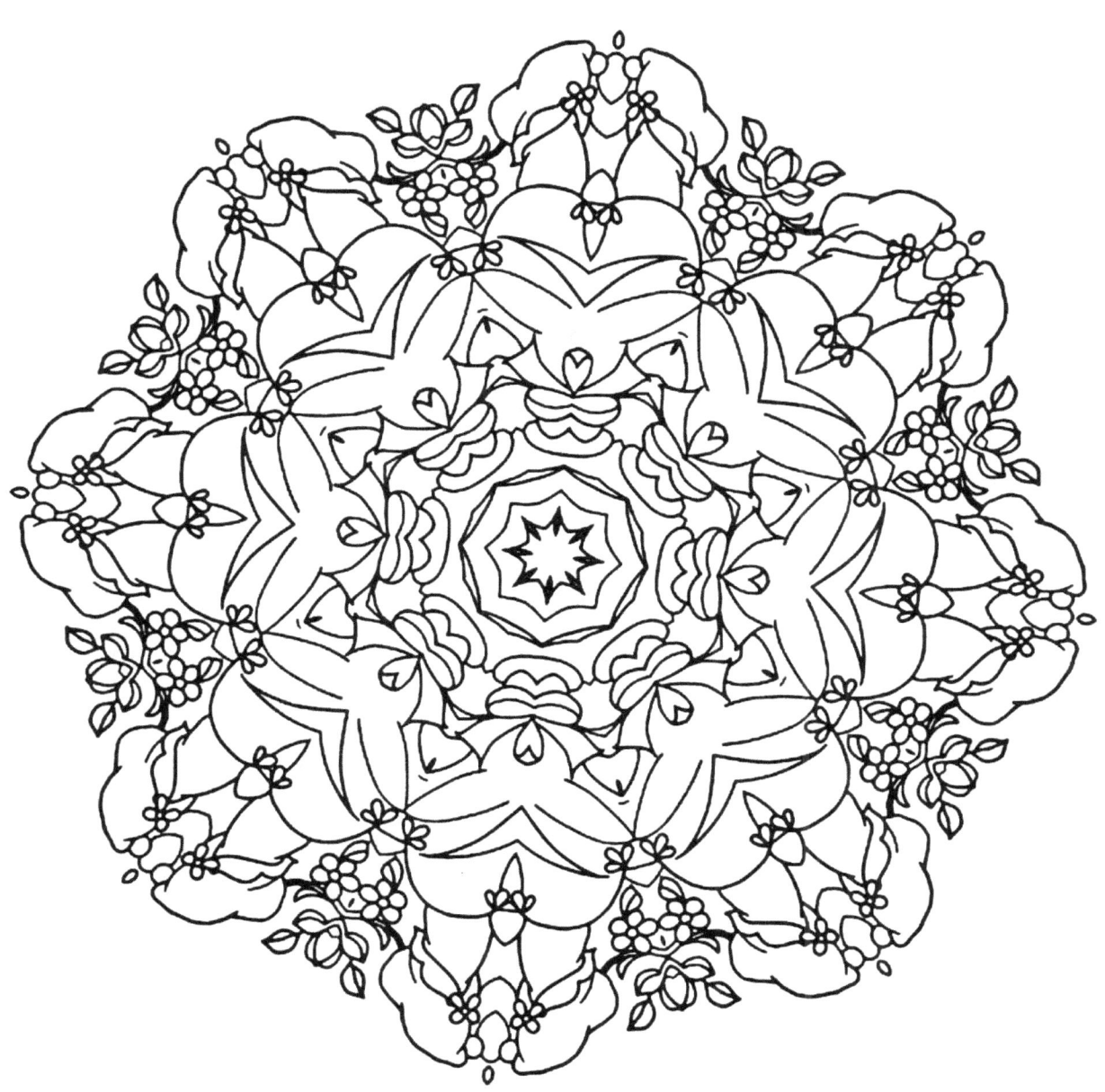

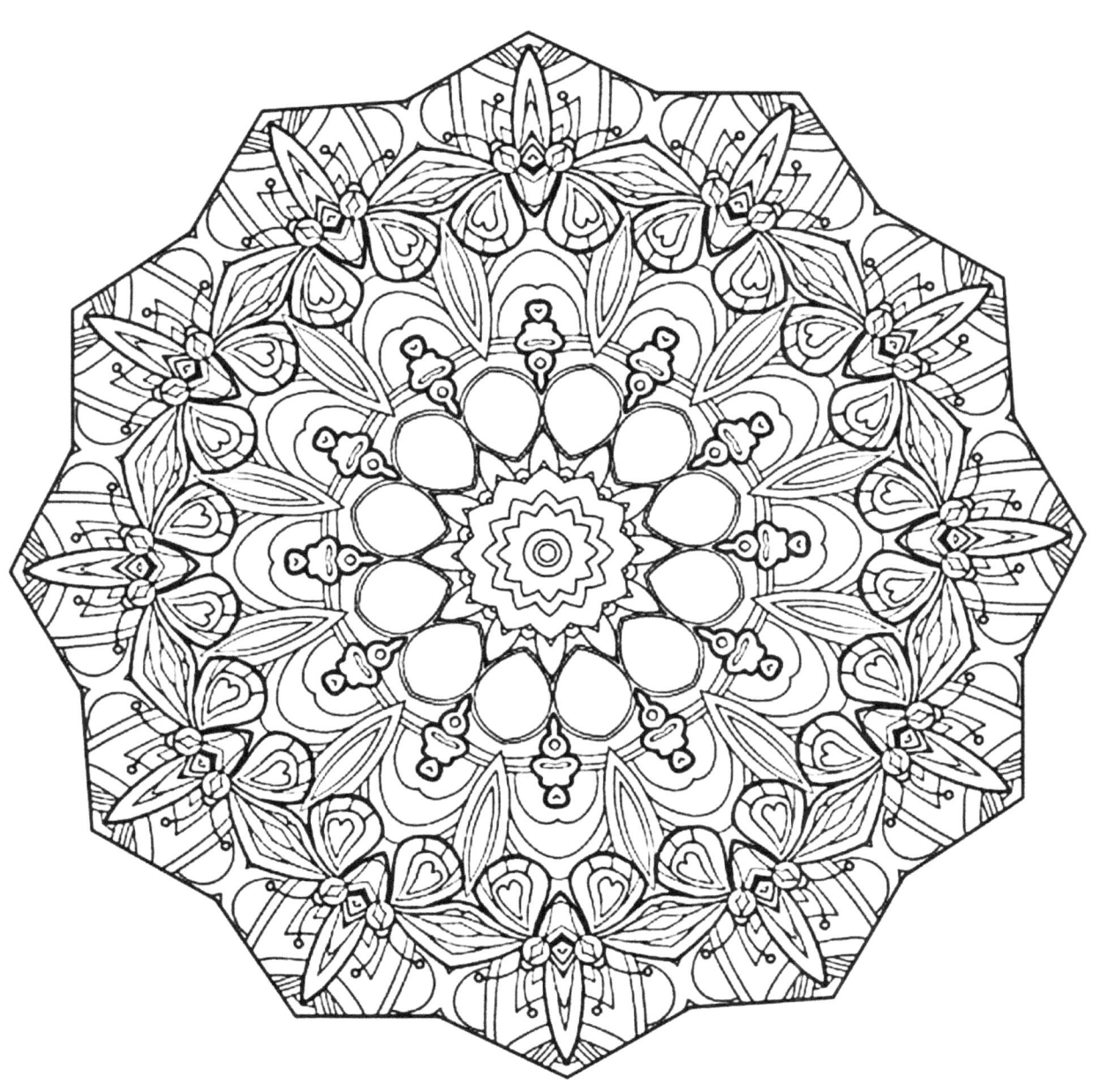

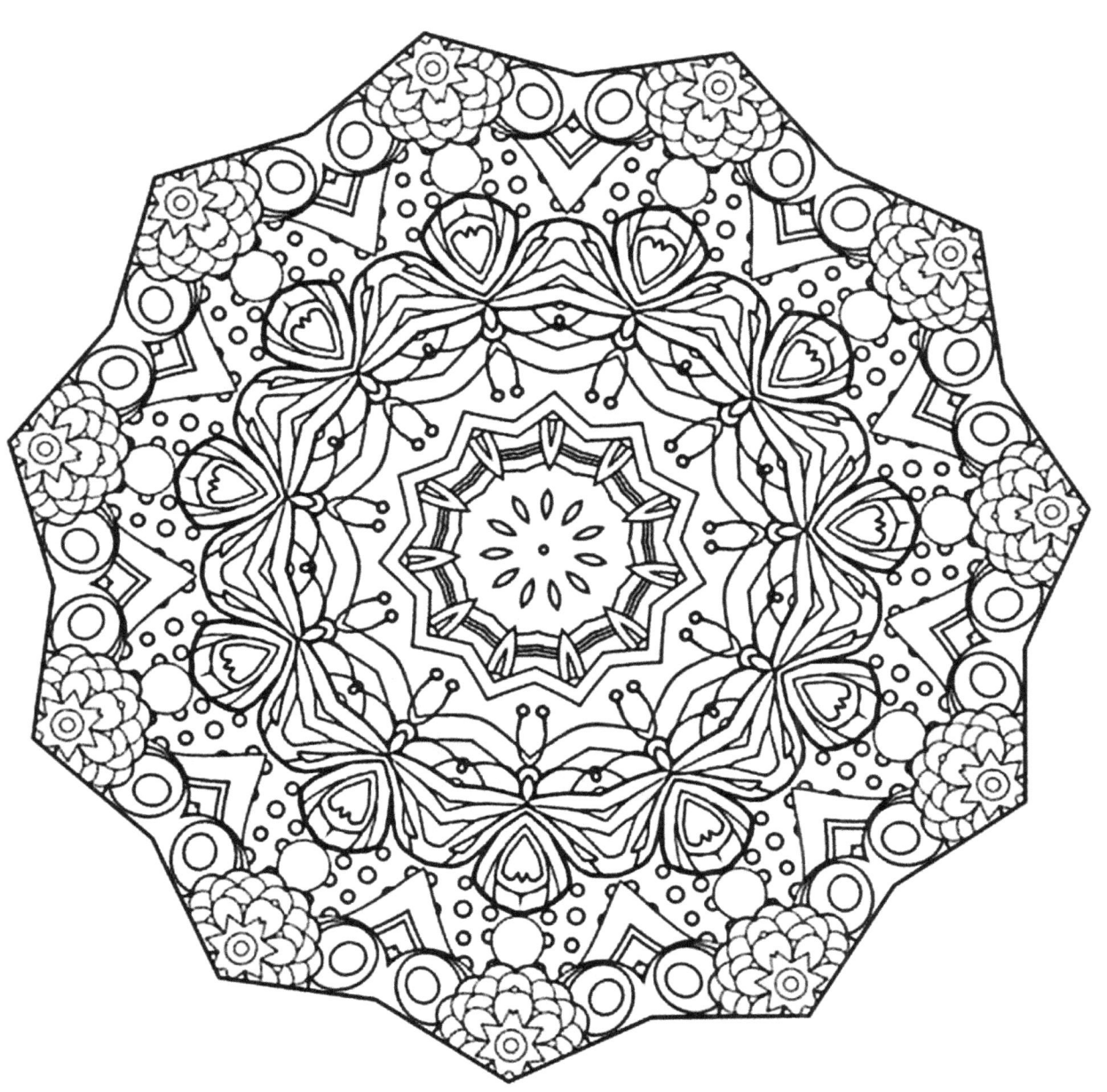

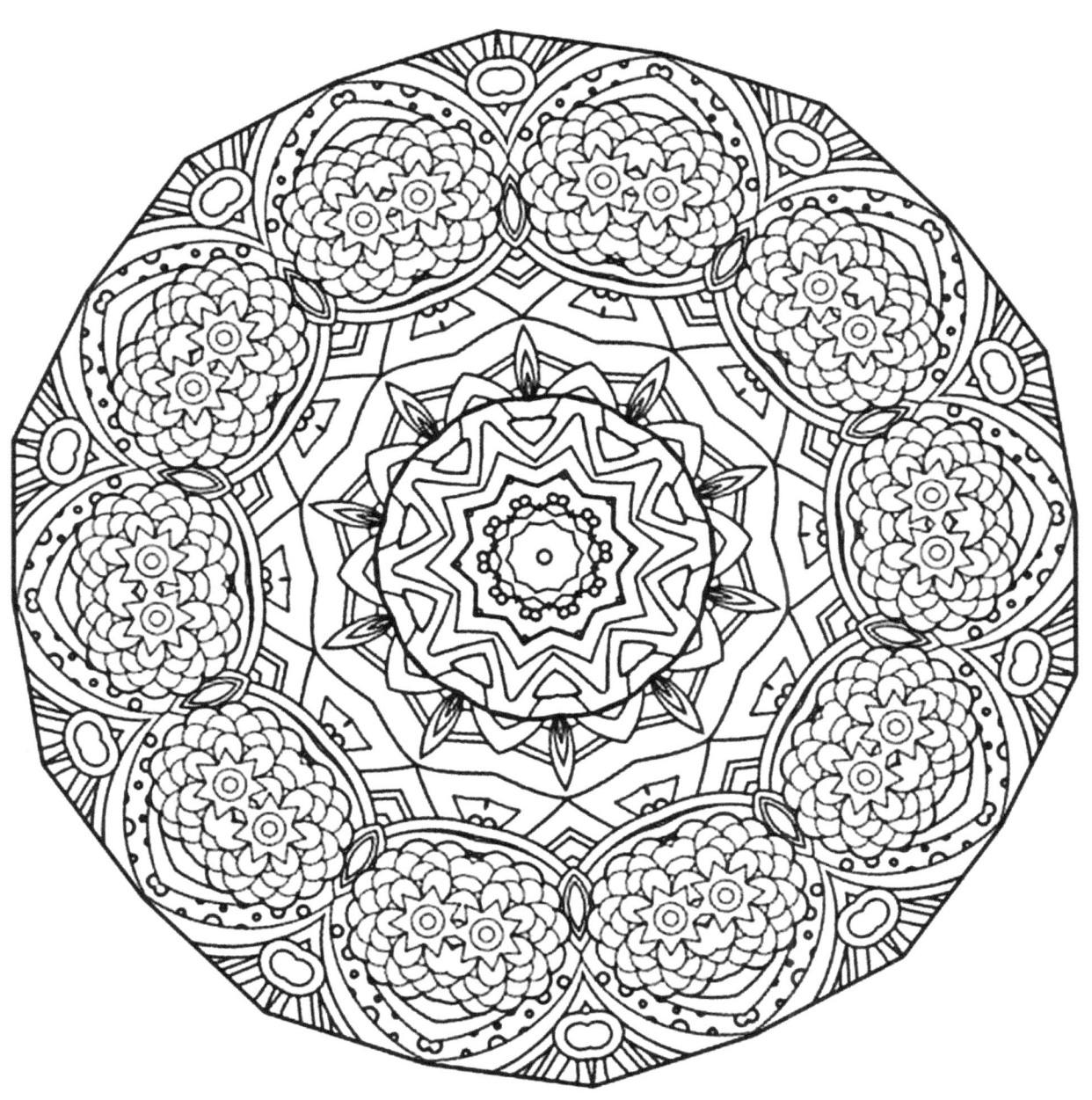

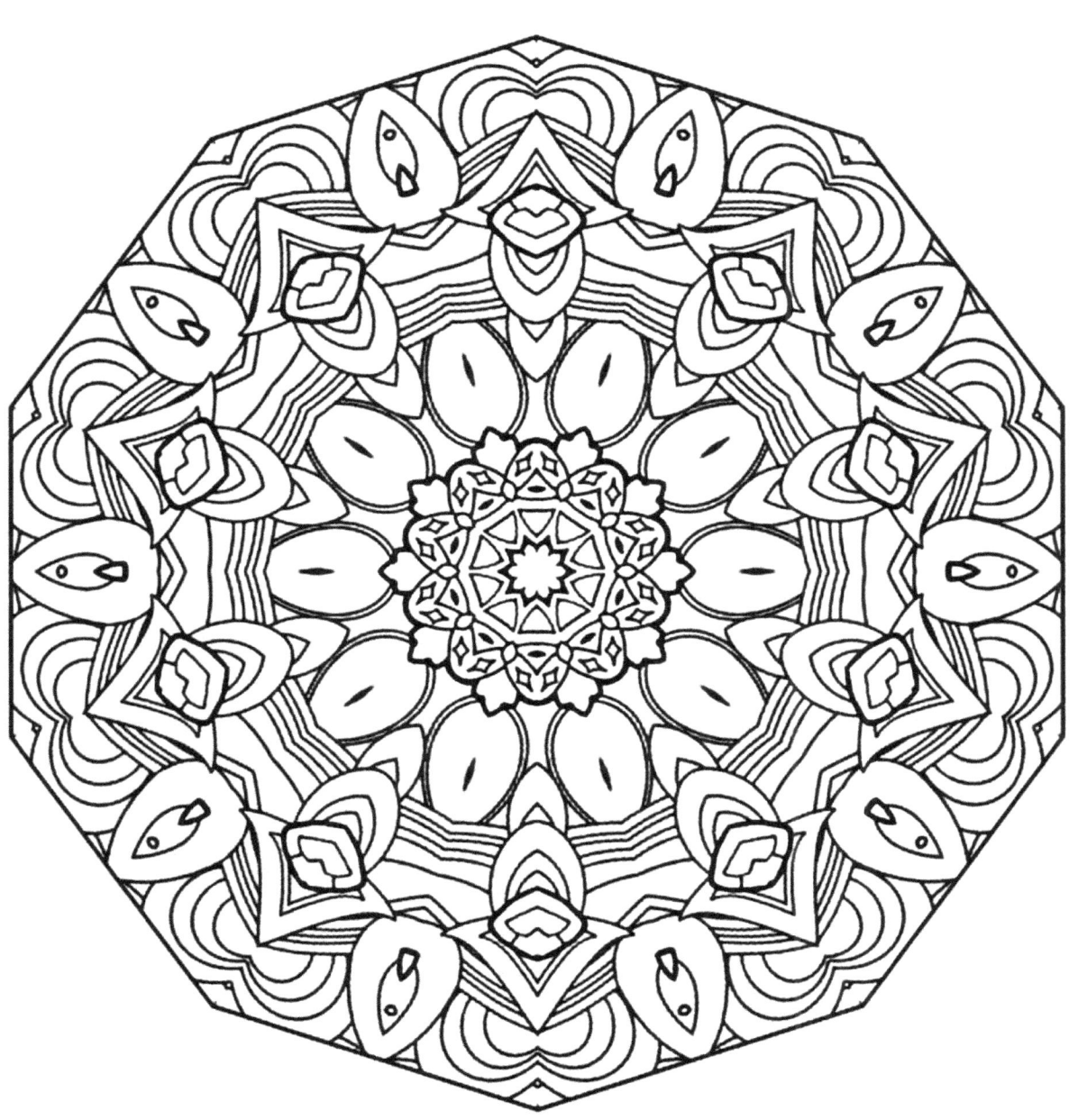

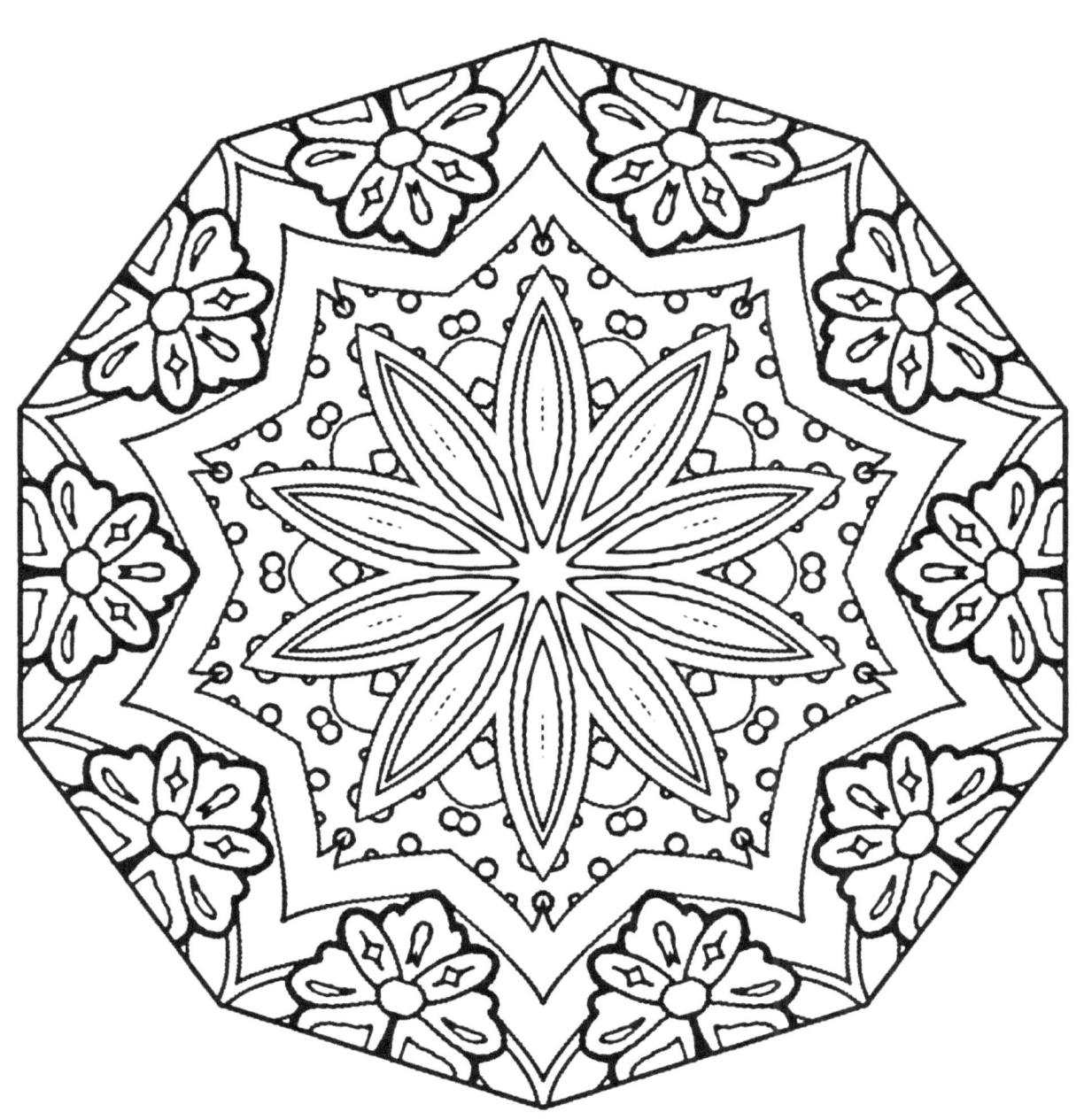

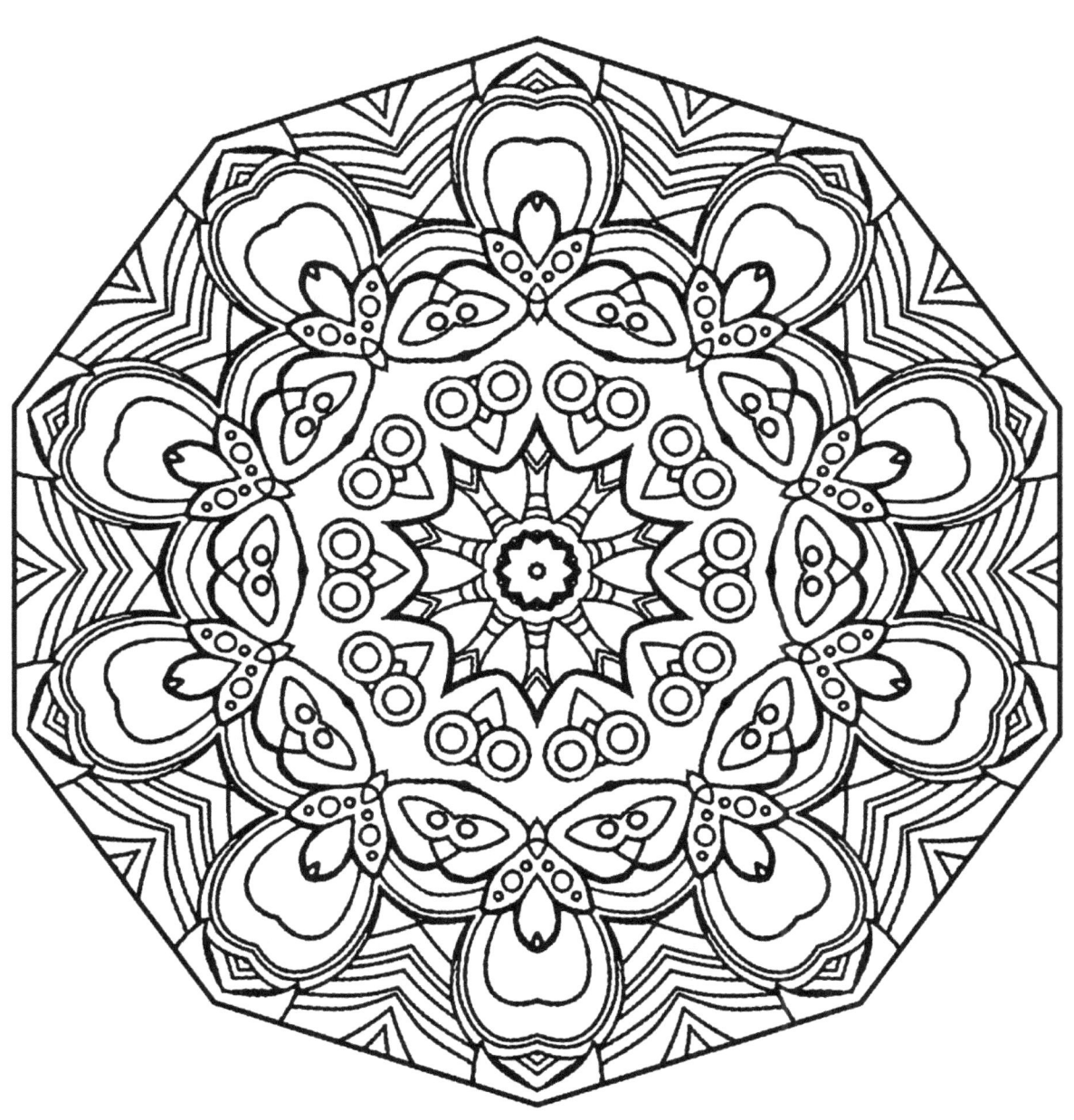

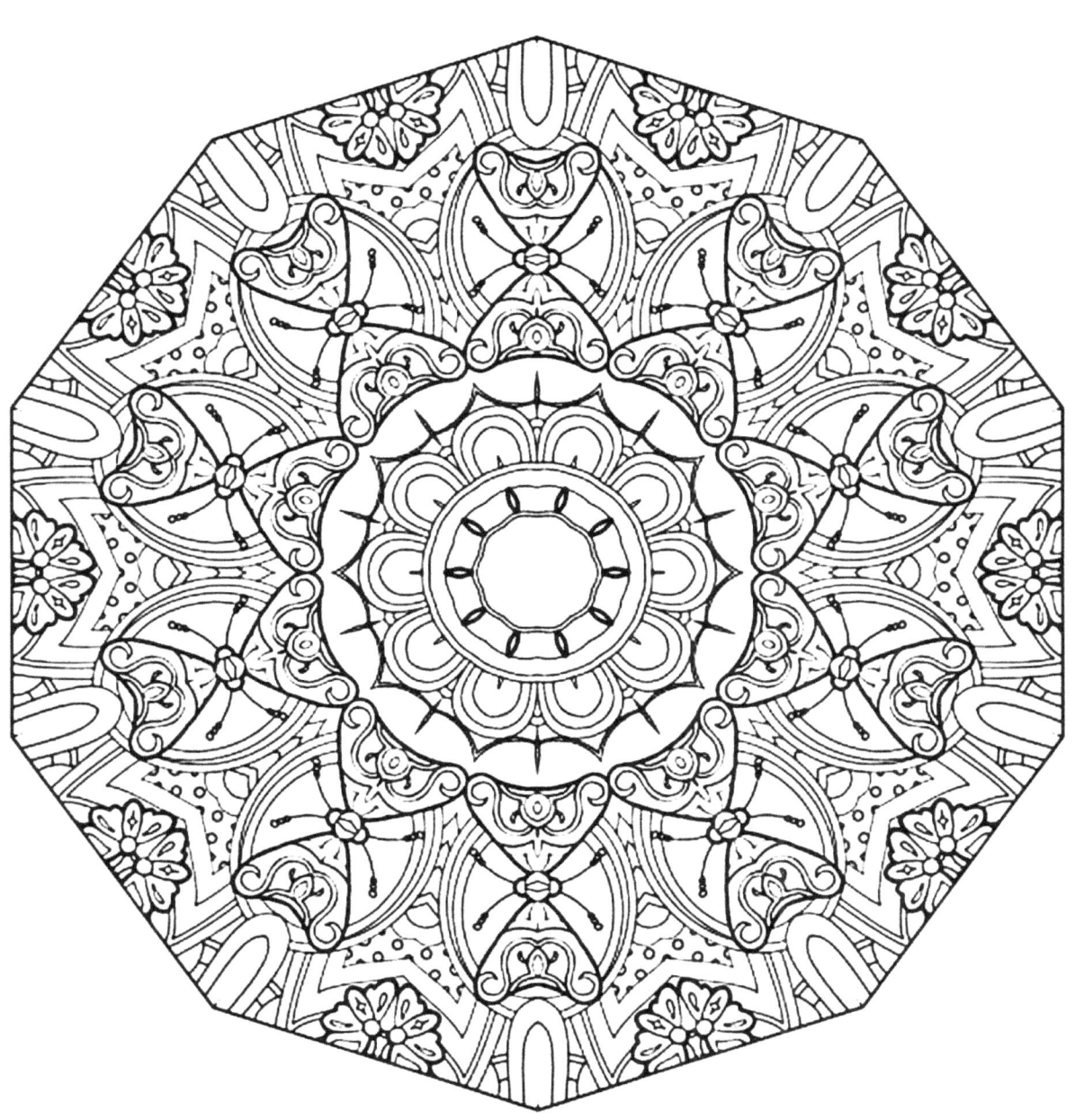

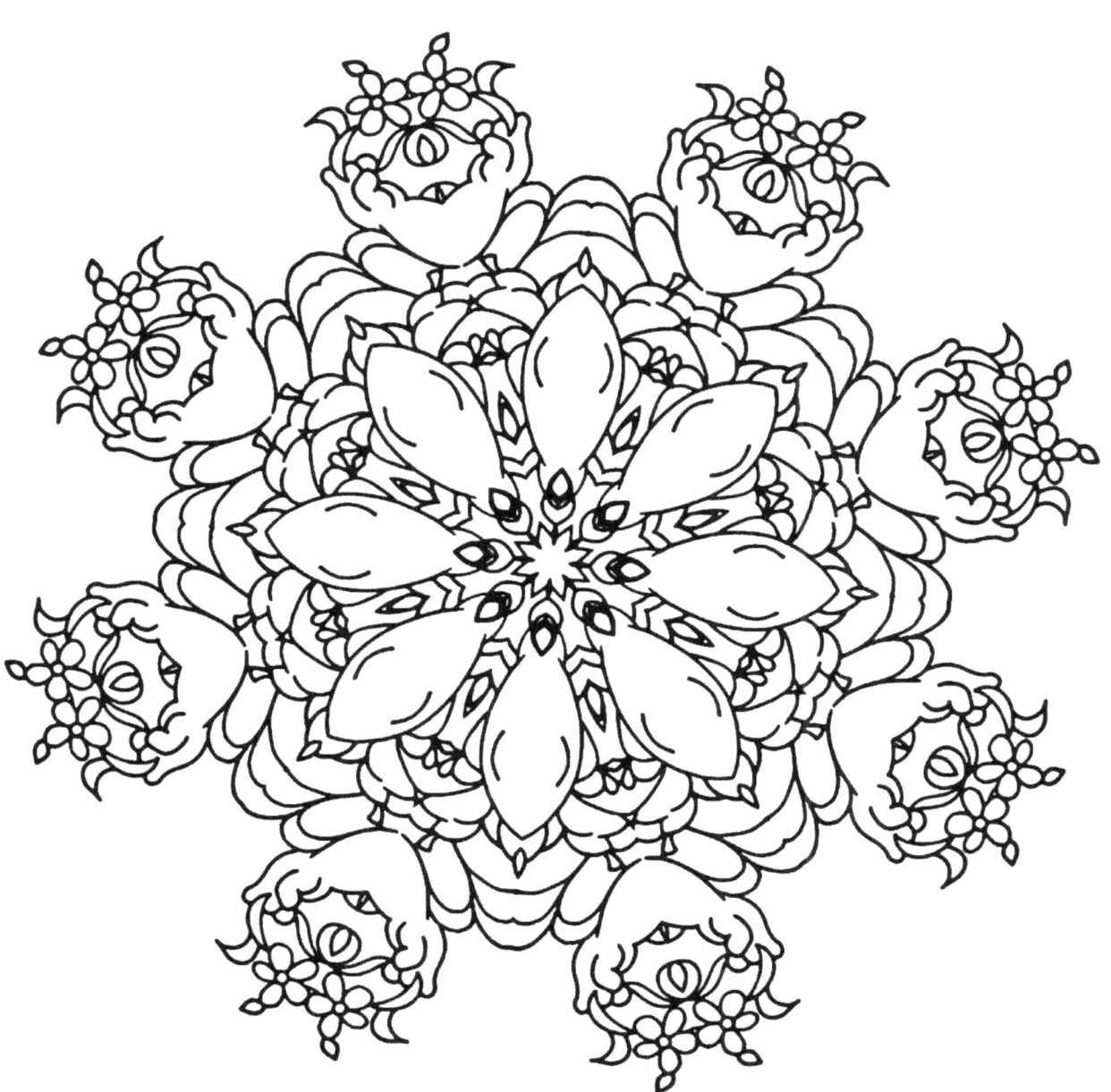

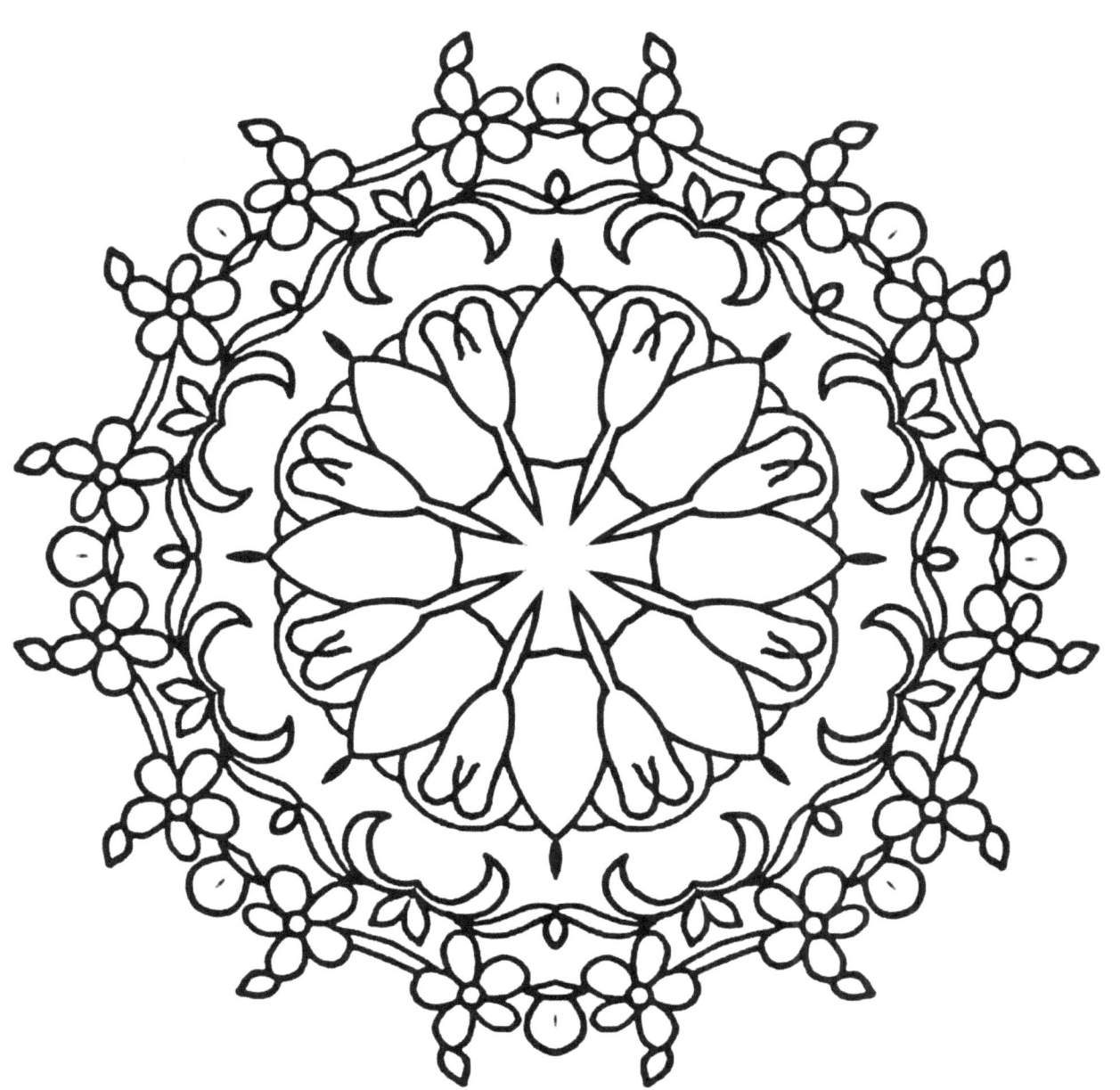

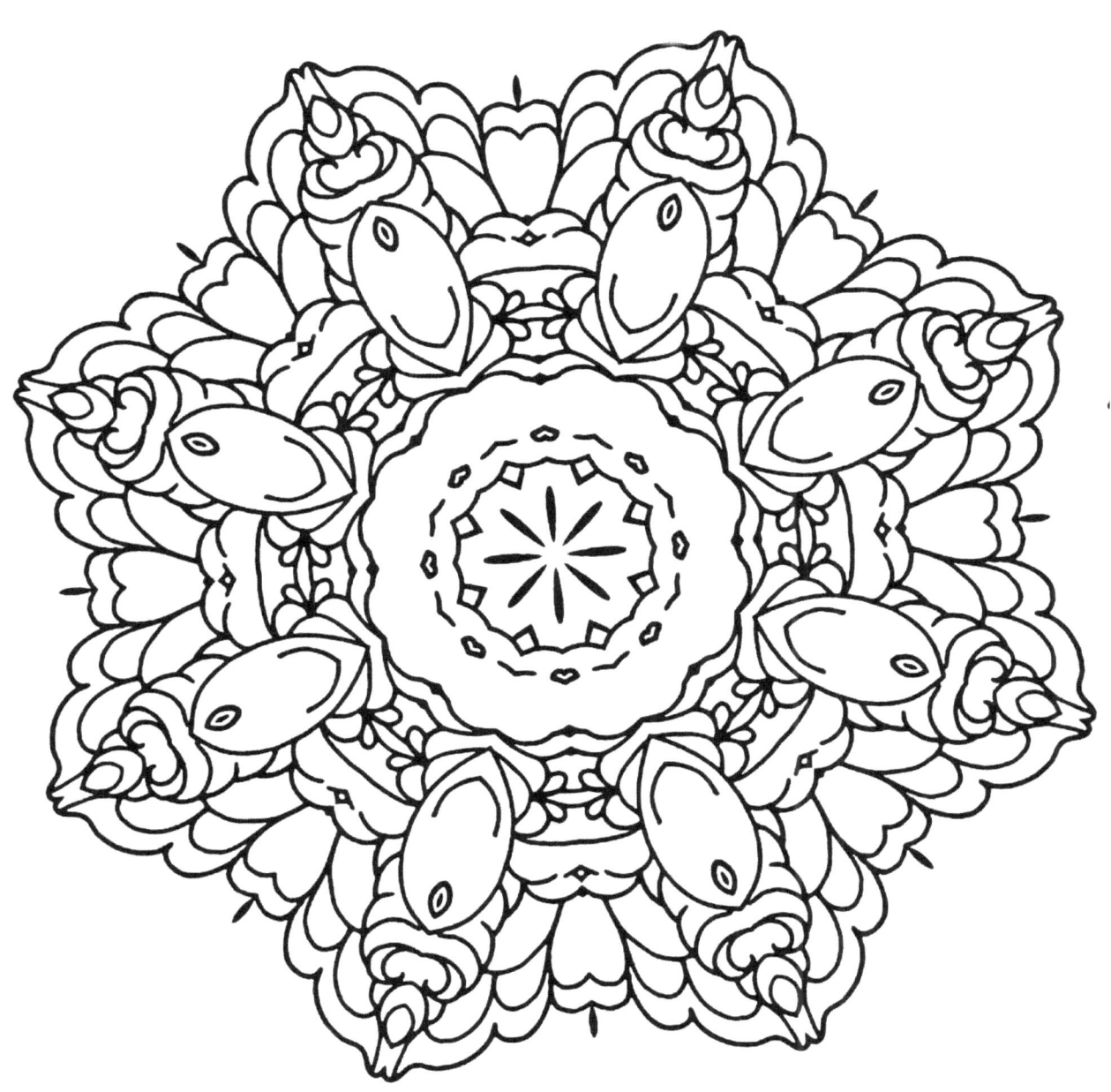

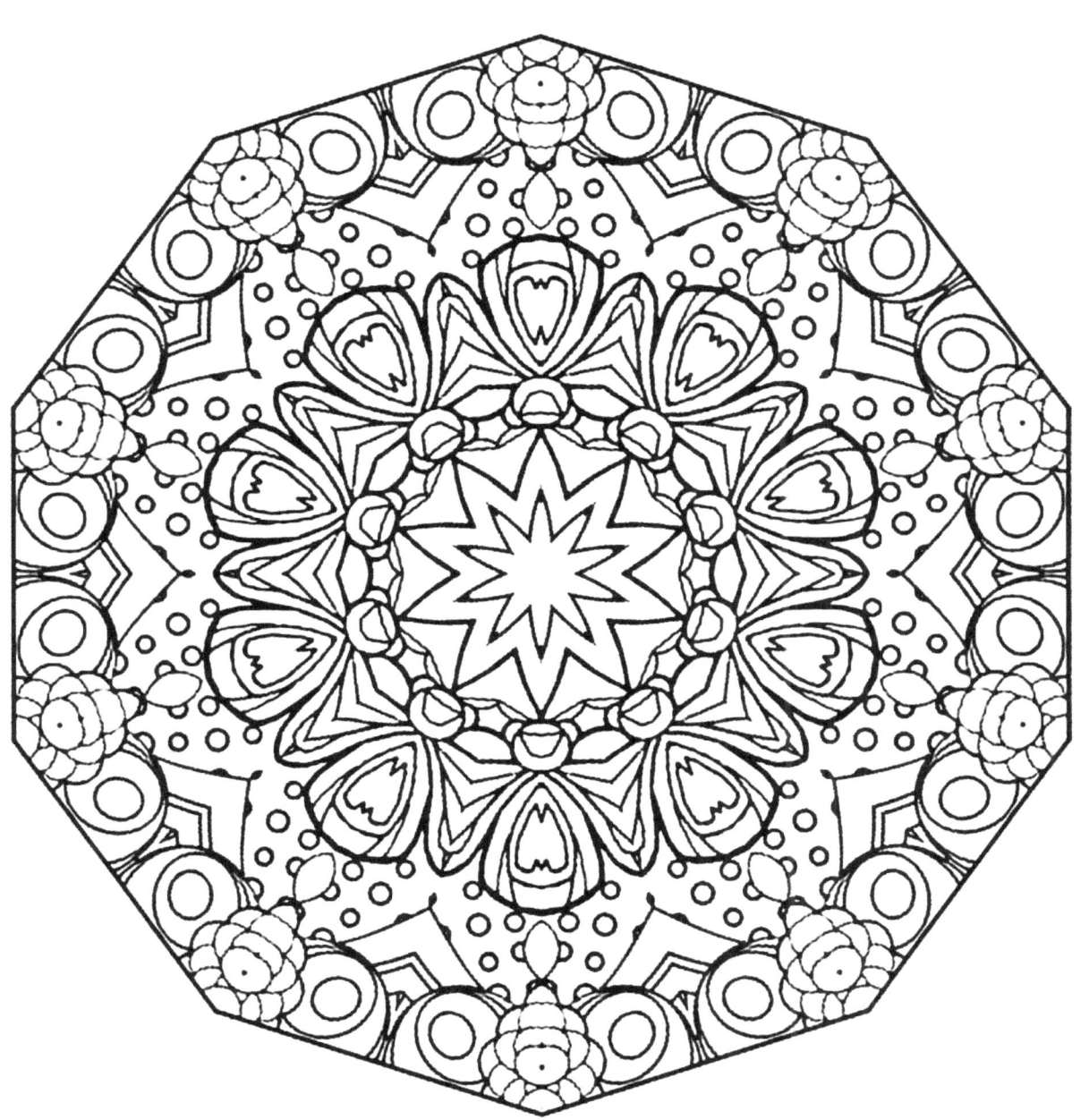

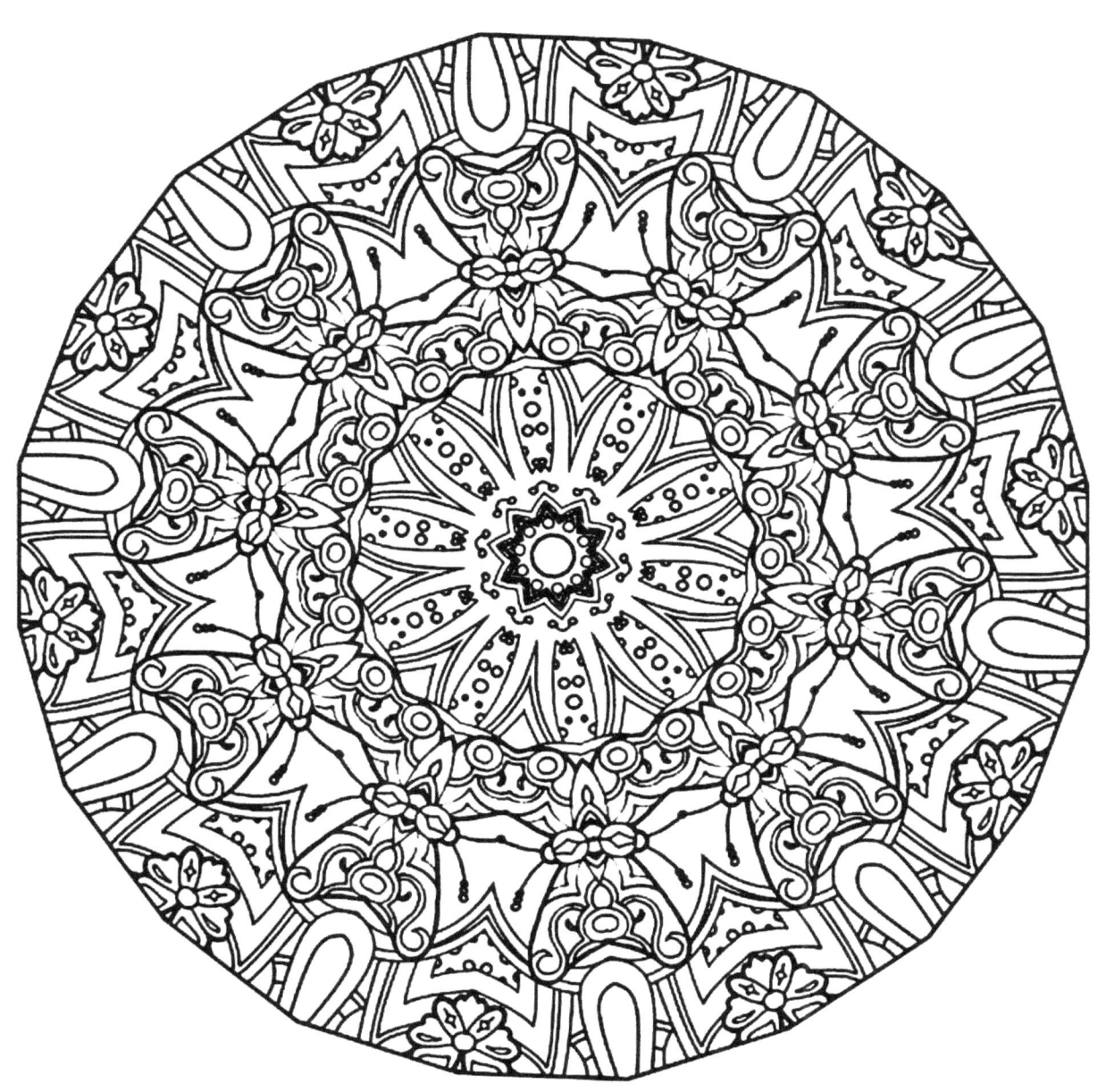

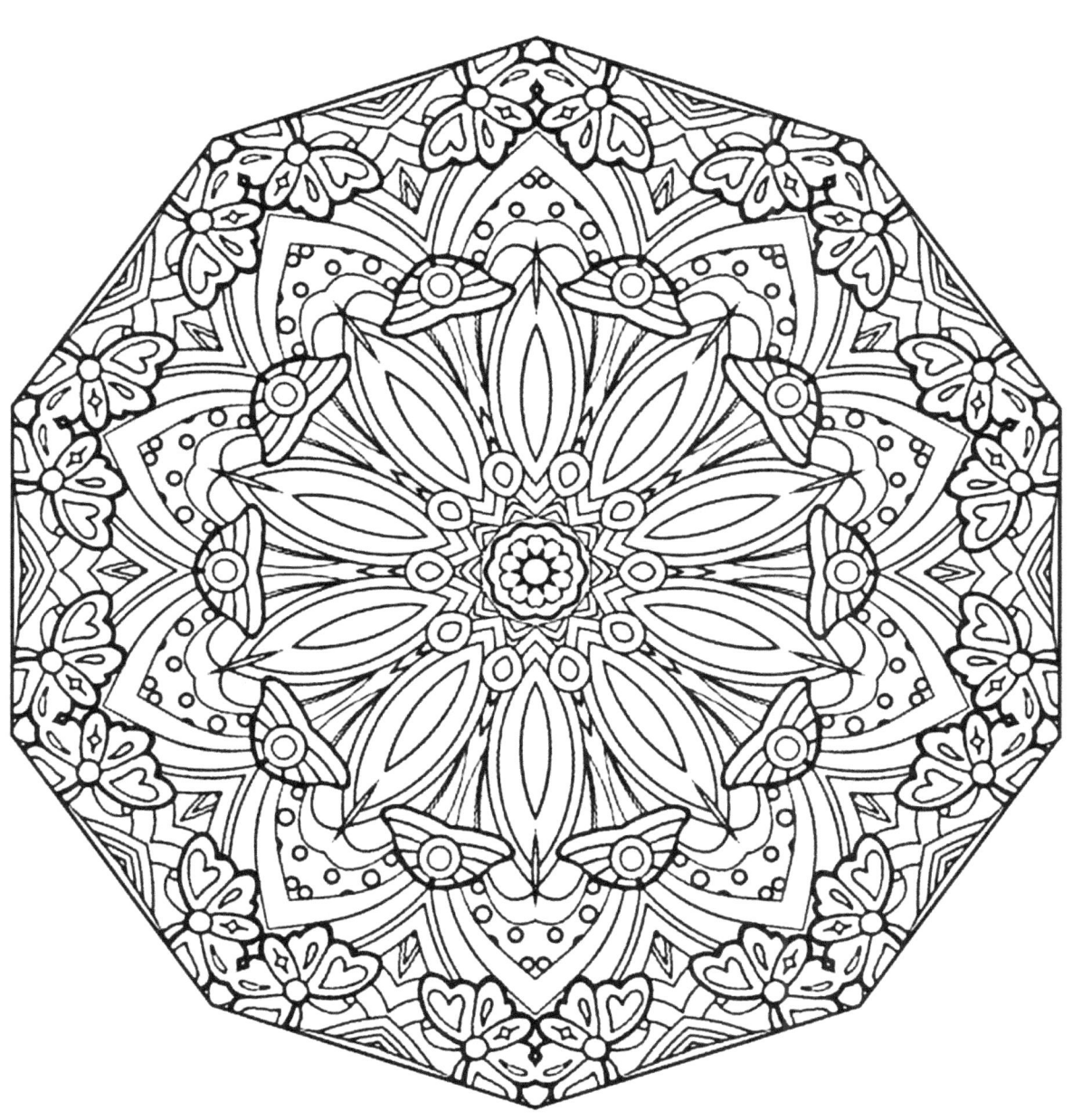

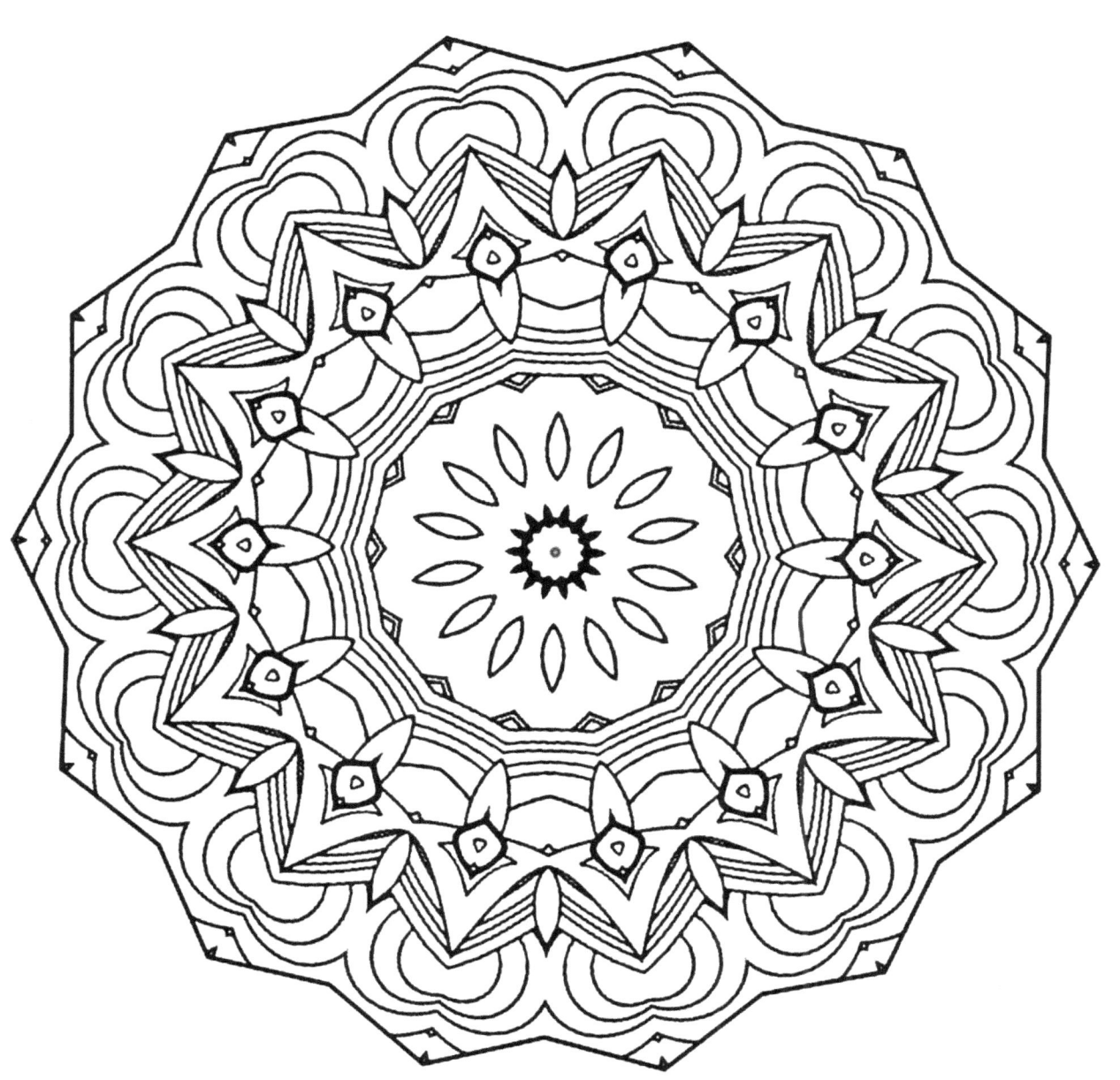

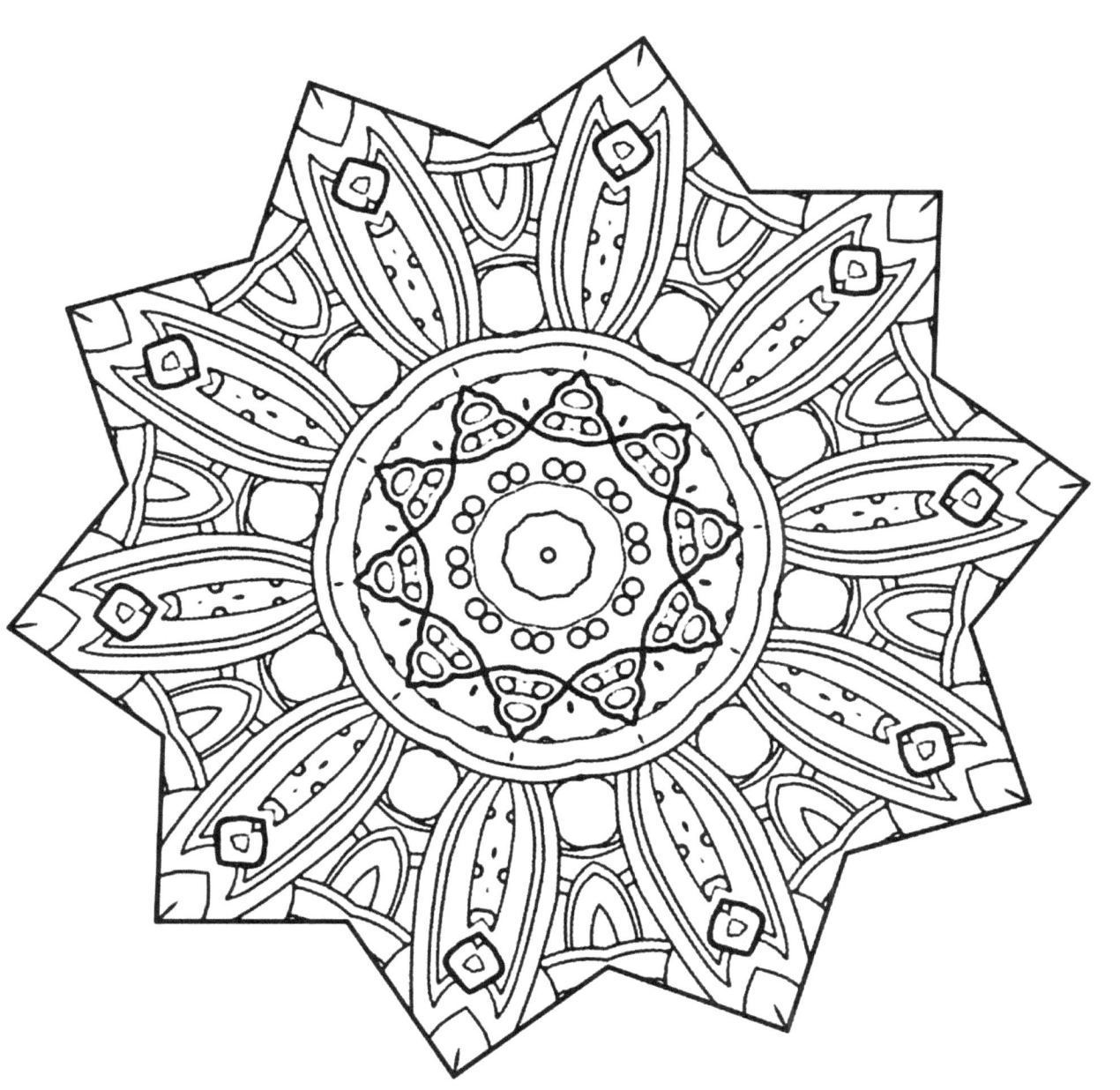

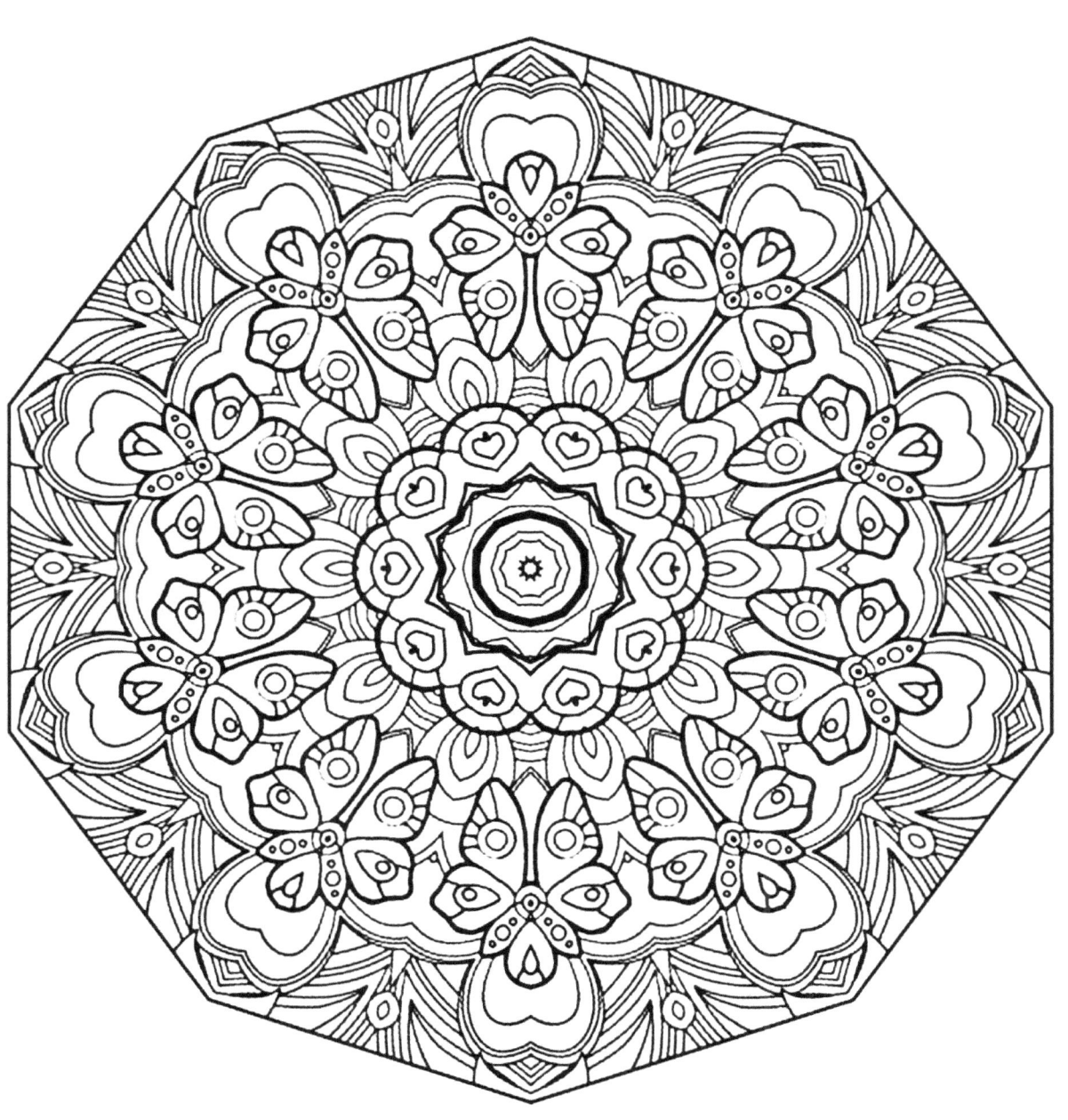

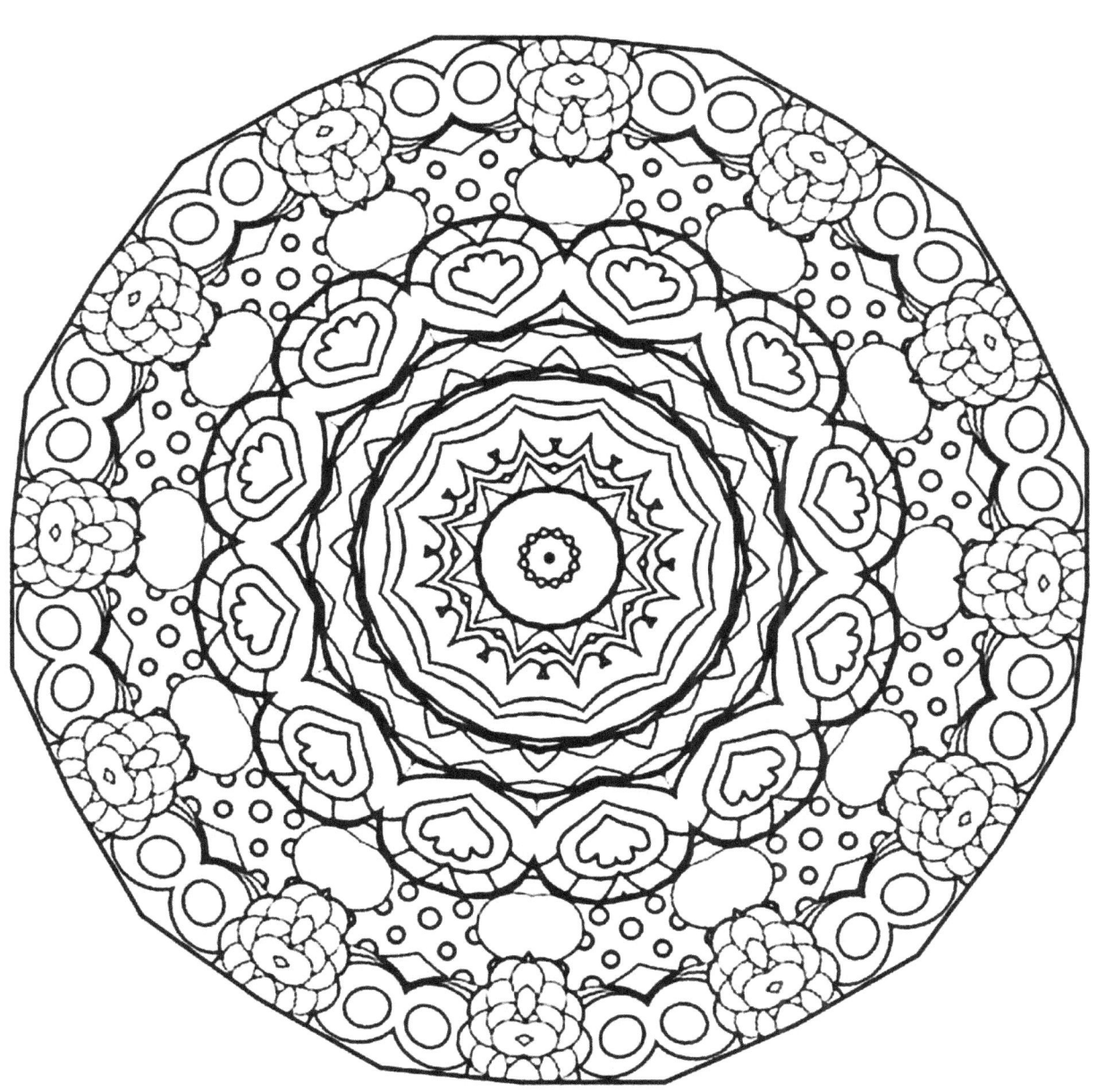

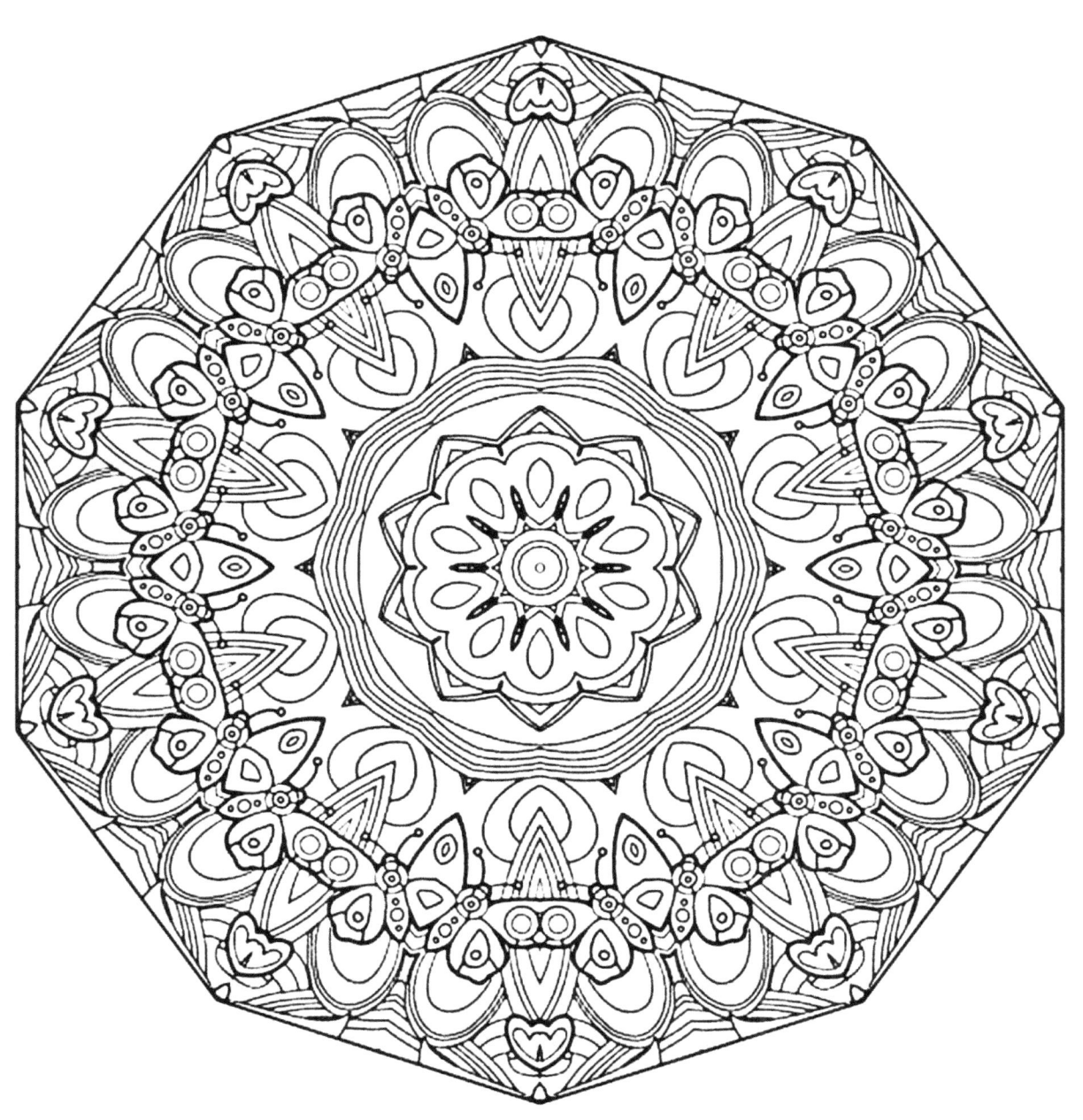

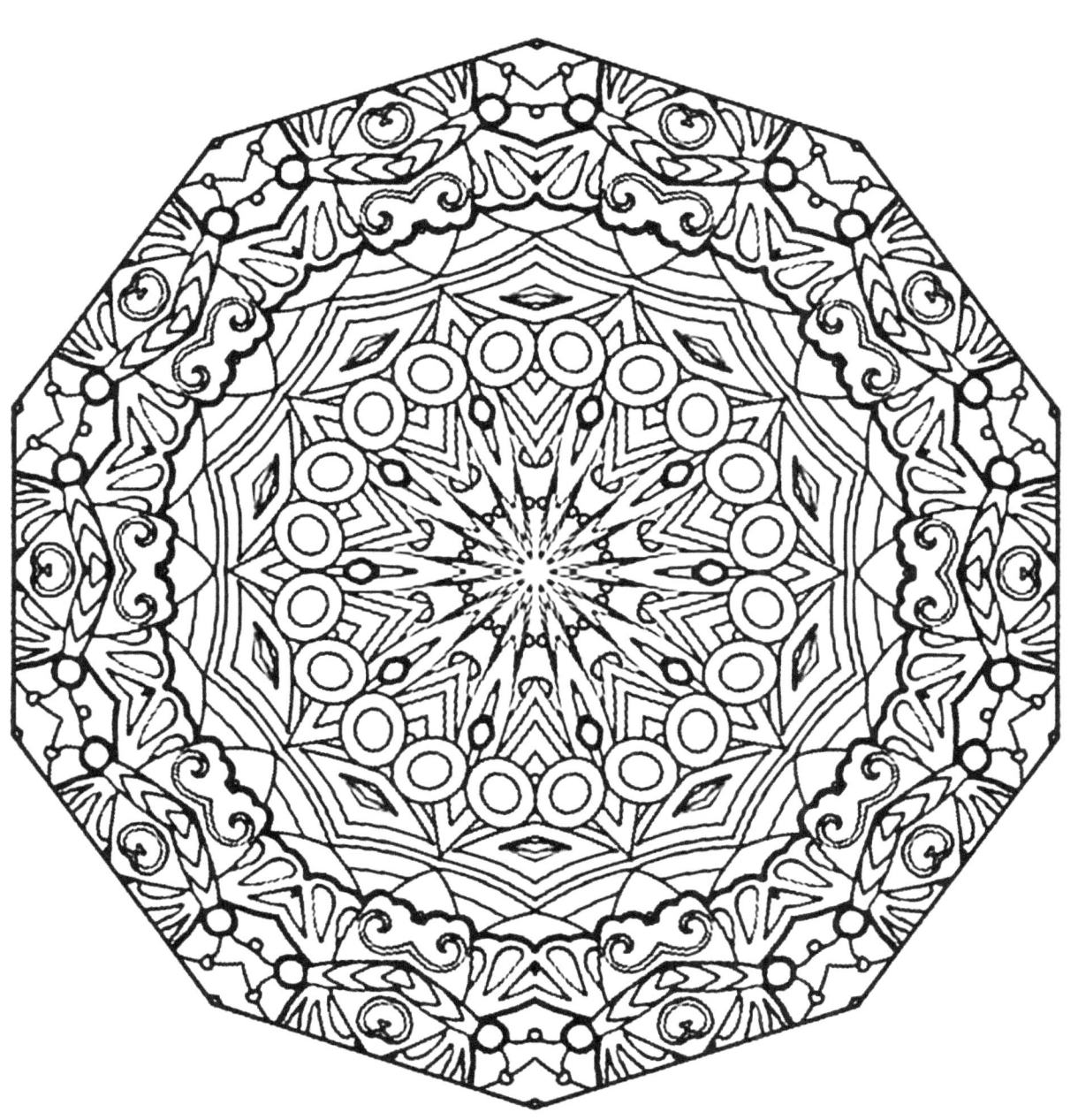

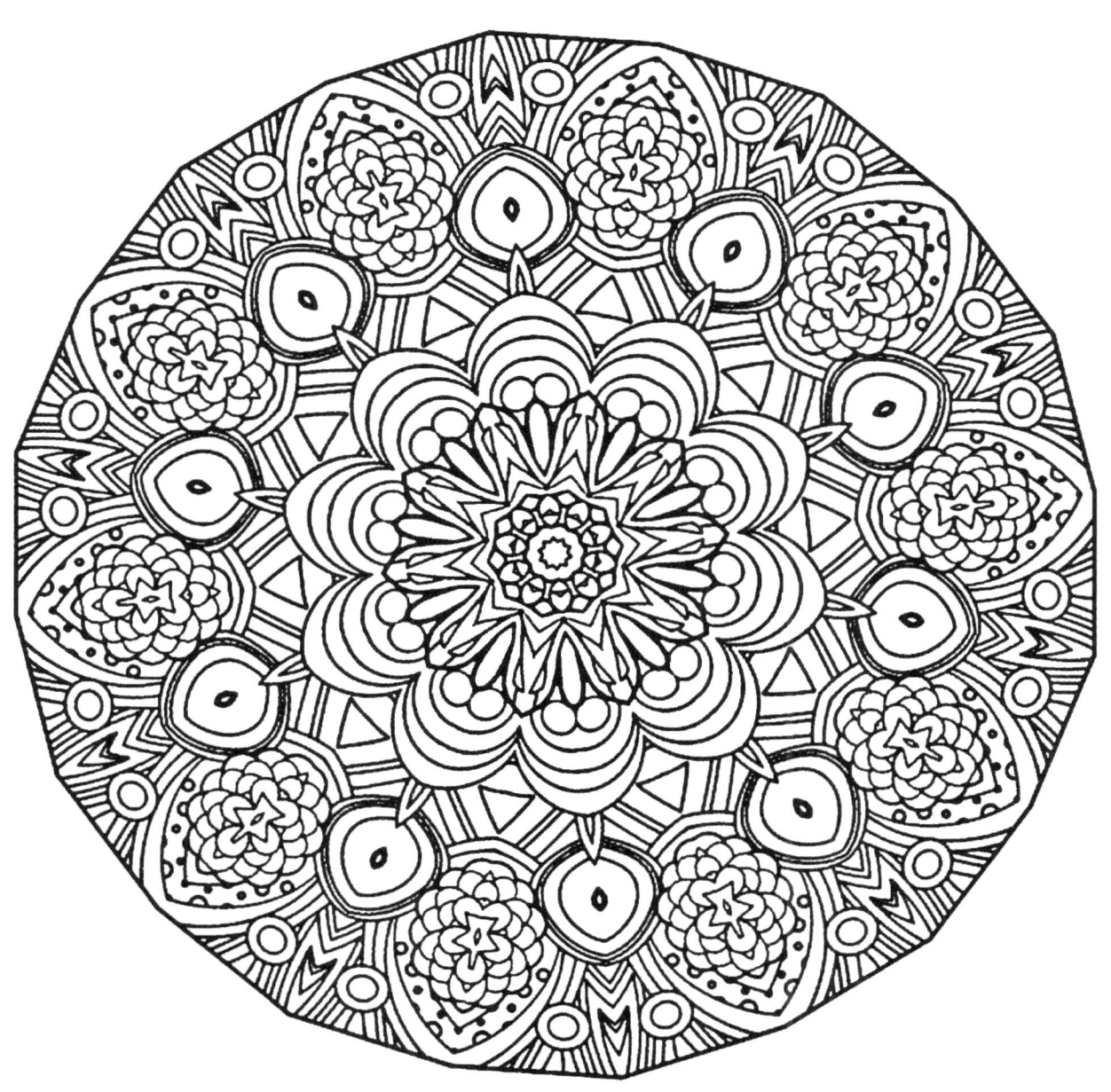

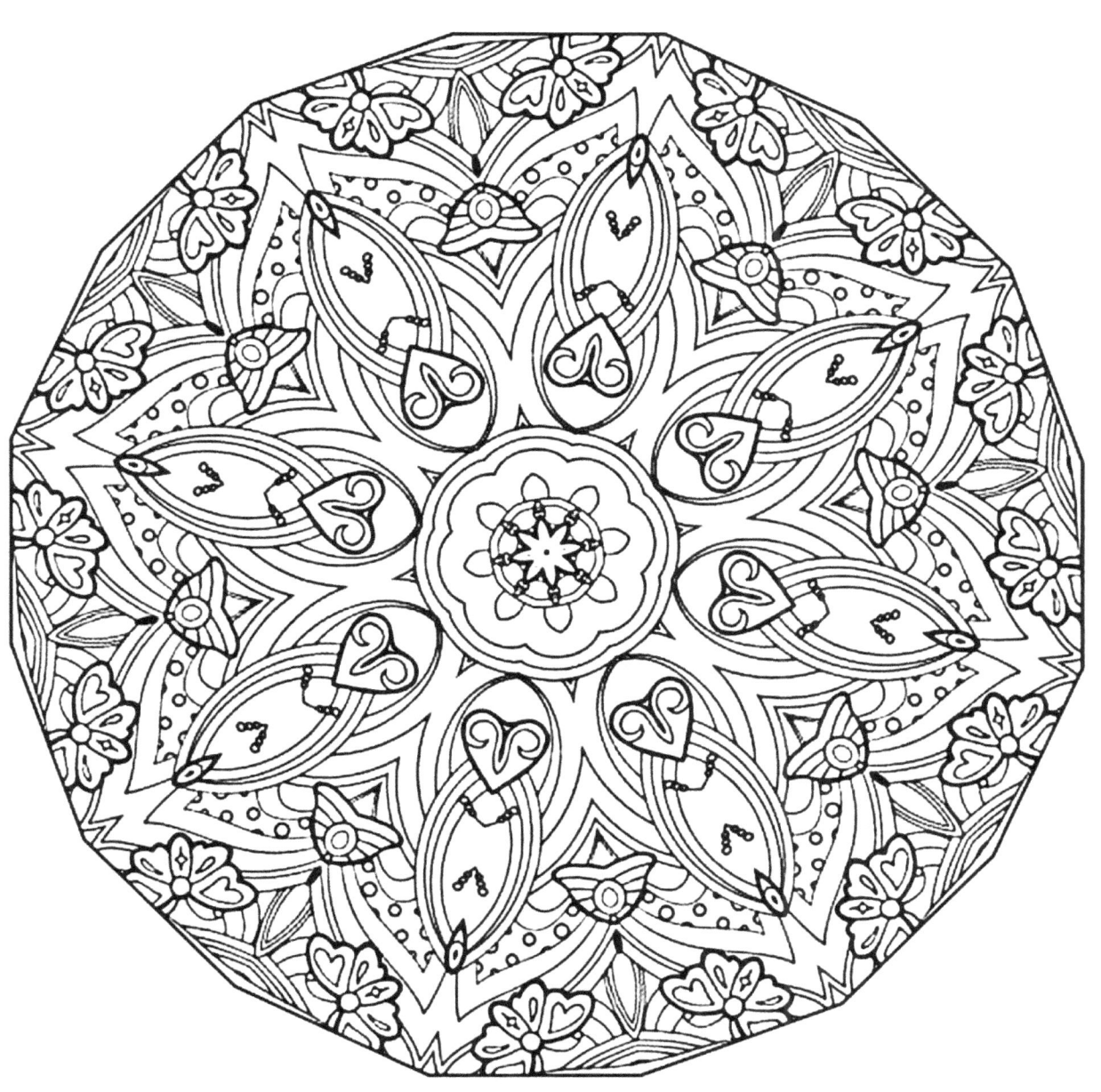

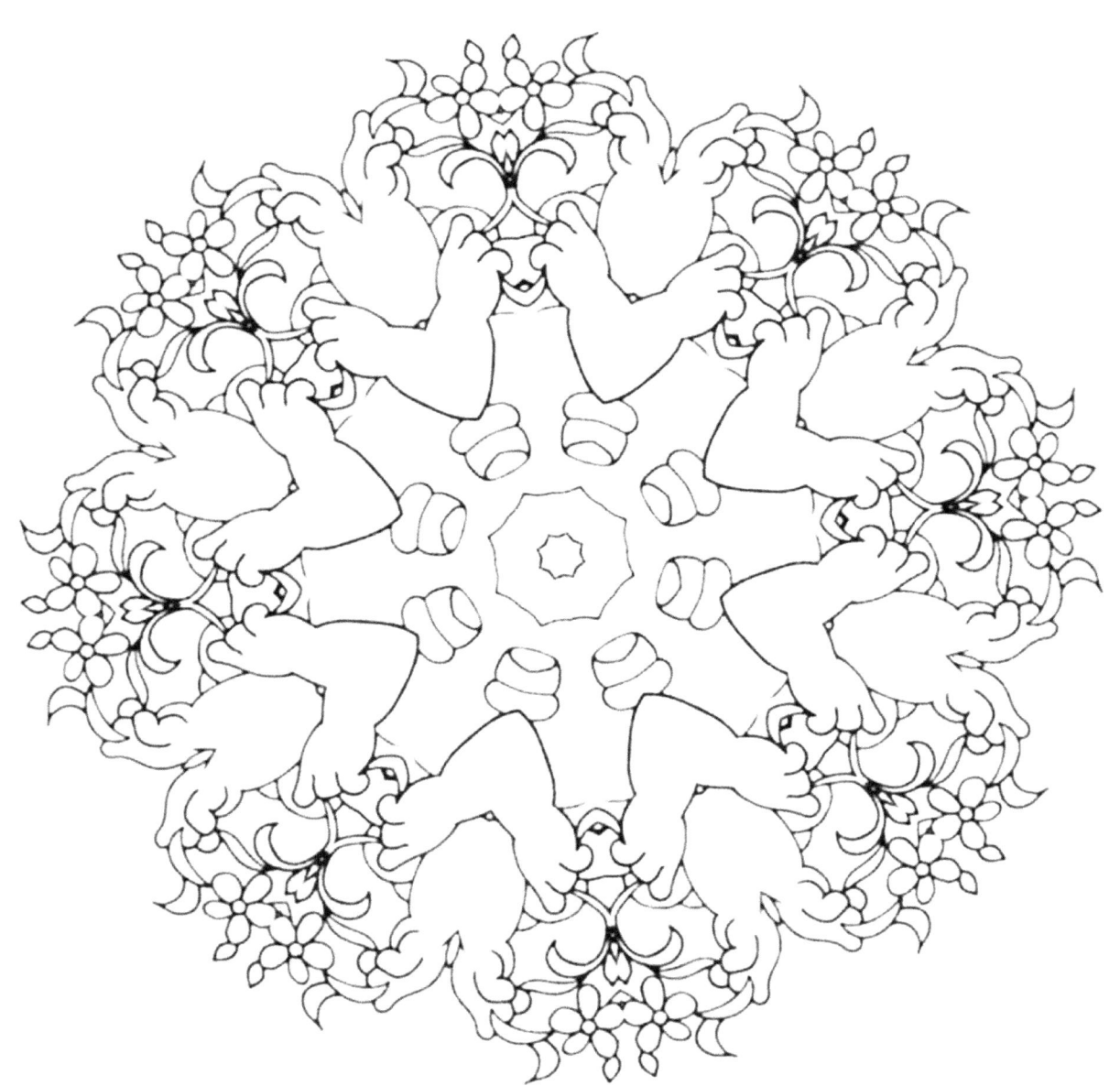

Thank you

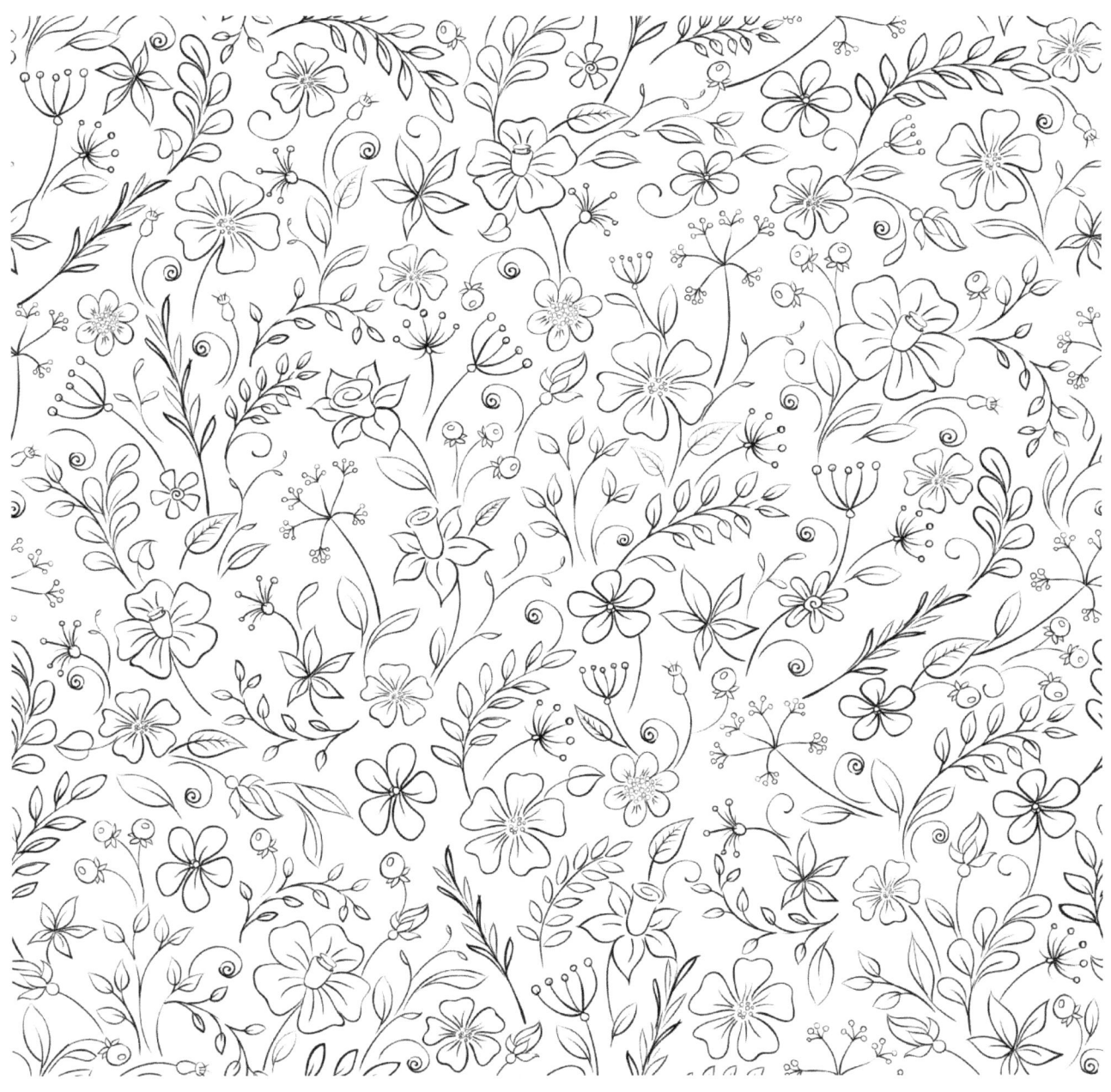

www.ingramcontent.com/pod-product-compliance
Lightning Source LLC
Chambersburg PA
CBHW081741170526
45167CB00009B/3903